THE INSTITUTE FOR SPECIES SYSTEMIZATION:

AN EXPERIMENTAL ARCHIVE

VOLUME ONE

PATRICIA ROSE

THE INSTITUTE FOR SPECIES SYSTEMIZATION:

AN EXPERIMENTAL ARCHIVE

VOLUME ONE

PATRICIA ROSE

**RESCUE
+PRESS**

Rescue Press, Milwaukee 53212
Copyright © 2011 by The Institute for Species Systemization
All rights reserved
Printed in the United States of America

www.rescue-press.org

Cover design by Skye McNeill
Book design by Rescue Press
First Edition

ISBN: 978-0-9844889-7-1

THE INSTITUTE FOR SPECIES SYSTEMIZATION:

AN EXPERIMENTAL ARCHIVE

ISS RESEARCH POLICIES

The Institute for Species Systemization (ISS) will comply with all provisions of the Animal Welfare Act.

The Institute is advised by the "U.S. Government Principles for the Utilization and Care of Vertebrate Animals used in Testing, Research, and Training."

The Institute maintains that animals may not be housed for more than twelve hours within designated testing areas without prior review and approval by the committee.

The Institute does not accept responsibility for the care and use of animals involved in testing, assuming that all consent forms are signed prior to examination.

The Institute requires that all animals are screened for physical abnormalities before entry into the testing site is permitted.

The Institute reserves the right to remove unruly animals from the premises.

The Institute requires that all personnel working with animals must be appropriately clothed and vaccinated.

Please contact the Compliance Manager at (414) 426-9218 if there are concerns regarding the humane care of subjects under the supervision of the ISS.

CONTENTS:

INTRODUCTION 3

TESTING SITE I 9

TESTING SITE II 29

TESTING SITE III 47

TESTING SITE IV 67

BIBLIOGRAPHY 81

BIOGRAPHY 83

INTRODUCTION

The Institute for Species Systemization (ISS) has been involved in scientific research and subject testing for over twenty-two years. This volume is an archive and collection of ISS studies to date and includes a sampling of preliminary and experimental analyses of the human species (our primary animal subjects). This introduction begins with a taxonomic listing of the species (according to the system initially established by Linnaeus) in order to contextualize the impetus of our studies and experimental philosophy.

Common Name: *Human*
Kingdom: *Animalia*
Phylum: *Chordata*
Class: *Mammalia*
Order: *Primata*
Family: *Hominidae*
Genus: *Homo*
Species: *Homo Sapiens*

In the current year, 2011, Homo Sapien Sapien, as named by human scientists, lives in almost every biome on planet Earth. Defining humans according to normal classifications such as diet, habitat, and social status is an impossible task due to the complexity and diversity of the species, as well as their systems of classification and description.

The human species' interest in and ability to classify the world around them is, of course, a large contributor to both their societal and cultural developments. For example, in early evolutionary times, defining specific foods and seasons were one method of organizing dietary information. The development of language has been a vital tool in communicating useful information, organizing groups, and expressing complex cognitive processes.

However, the species' taxonomic proficiency has also been utilized in unethical ways, as a means to create superficial distinctions between groups via language, both within the species and directed at other animals. The species often makes inaccurate linguistic distinctions, excluding themselves from the animal kingdom. This may be due in part to their highly advanced technological innovations and the tendency of many members of the species to treat other animals as mechanisms.

While researching and examining complex illustrations of human evolution it became clear to the ISS that human ancestry is in many ways extraordinarily distant from other animals even though genetically the species is very closely related to other anthropoids. That said, the ISS is convinced that it is important when studying a specimen to maintain a certain level of objectivity, and the ISS in every scenario has attempted to consider the species based on detailed component parts in order to build an accurate data set.

Although all researchers at the Institute are members of the human species, our commitment to unbiased observation prohibits us from injecting personal accounts into this archive, to the best of each researcher's ability. Maintaining a level of neutrality and taking neither an '*anthropomorphic*' nor an '*anthropocentric*' viewpoint is a part of our process at the ISS.

The ISS is primarily interested in studying the human species in order to question the linguistic difficulties and gestures that describe and define how the species understands or interacts within the world. The probative process of our psychological experiments is necessary so that we may better understand the species' interest in power dynamics and social interactions, specist or exclusive language practice, and also as a broad phenomenological examination of complex organisms.

NOTES ON CONSENT AND DATA COMPILATION

NOTE 1: The Institute and its affiliates assume no liability for distributing information provided by subjects that did not sign or thoroughly review the informed consent materials distributed at all ISS testing sites. It was made clear to the subjects that upon entering the testing sites they surrendered their rights and therefore would be unable to defend their position in a court of law. In addition to the signature line on the *Subject Surveys* and the *Informed Consent* forms, signage was posted outside of the testing sites. Each stated:

Thank you for taking the time to participate. Your efforts will enable the Institute for Species Systemization (ISS) to continue its research, without which these studies could not be possible.

Please note: Subject participation is voluntary. By entering the testing site you are agreeing to participate in the study and all of its components. You are also acknowledging that the organizers will not be held liable for any complications or damages that may arise as a result of the experiment. All observable data will be recorded and analyzed by ISS Researchers.

This project is funded by the Institute for Species Systemization. Contact our head researcher, Patricia Rose, to learn more about our studies, or visit our website at: www.instituteforspeciesystemization.org. To report concerns about our studies or the treatment of animals within ISS testing sites, please contact the Compliance Manager at: (414) 426-9218.

NOTE 2: ISS Researchers, Workers, and Monitors were required to directly transcribe subject responses without interfering with the data. Correcting spelling, capitalization, punctuation, or any other grammatical errors was strictly prohibited by the Institute.

TESTING SITE I

PROXIMITY MAINTENANCE

EXPERIMENT DESCRIPTION

TESTING SITE I was created by the ISS to examine animal behavior within unusual social and environmental circumstances.

Subjects were required to complete a *Subject Survey* in which they classified themselves as a part of the human species, explicated their preferred method of communication, and listed other taxonomic characteristics or personality traits.

Each subject was socially isolated while locked within the testing site for three minutes. A viewing window created a physical barrier between the researcher or monitor and subjects. The monitor verbally reported behavioral observations while subjects reacted to each situational variable.

Harry Harlow's studies in attachment theory were, in part, the initial impetus for TESTING SITE I. As in Harlow's studies, subjects were isolated and a distinct barrier was installed to prevent any physical interaction with the monitor. In this scenario, subjects were carefully analyzed. Specimens responded in primordial ways to a social scenario where it was made obvious through physical cues that researchers were observing and analyzing all behavioral responses.

PRECEDENT

Harry Harlow (1905—1981) was a psychologist who conducted experiments on rhesus monkeys at the University of Wisconsin—Madison in the 1960s. Harlow's most famous study involved two surrogates: one composed of metal and one composed of terrycloth. His findings indicated that rhesus infants clung to the terrycloth surrogate despite the fact that the metal surrogate was the infant's food source. When the infants were frightened by instigating mechanisms created by other scientists, they cowered and shook, looking for comfort in the precise spot where the cloth surrogate was previously located. Harlow wrote an article entitled "The Nature of Love," first published in *American Psychologist* in 1958, in which he stated: "We had also discovered during some allied observational studies that a baby monkey raised on a bare wire mesh cage floor survives with difficulty, if at all, during the first five days of life." Harlow's controversial psychological studies were conducted on unconsenting participants as a way of understanding the subjects' reaction to environmental situations and their need for survival in direct competition with emotional desires.

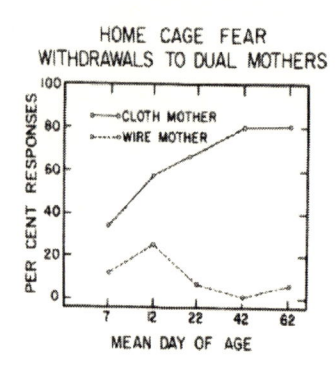

NOTE: This figure is a diagram from Harlow's "The Nature of Love."

Figure 15. Differential ness in fear tests.

RECEPTION

In TESTING SITE I, participants were received by a monitor who instructed them to complete a *Subject Survey*. After the proper paperwork was completed, subjects were issued an identification badge and asked to wait quietly in a *Reception Area* (below) until their number was called.

Subjects individually entered the testing site once instructed by *Monitor One*.

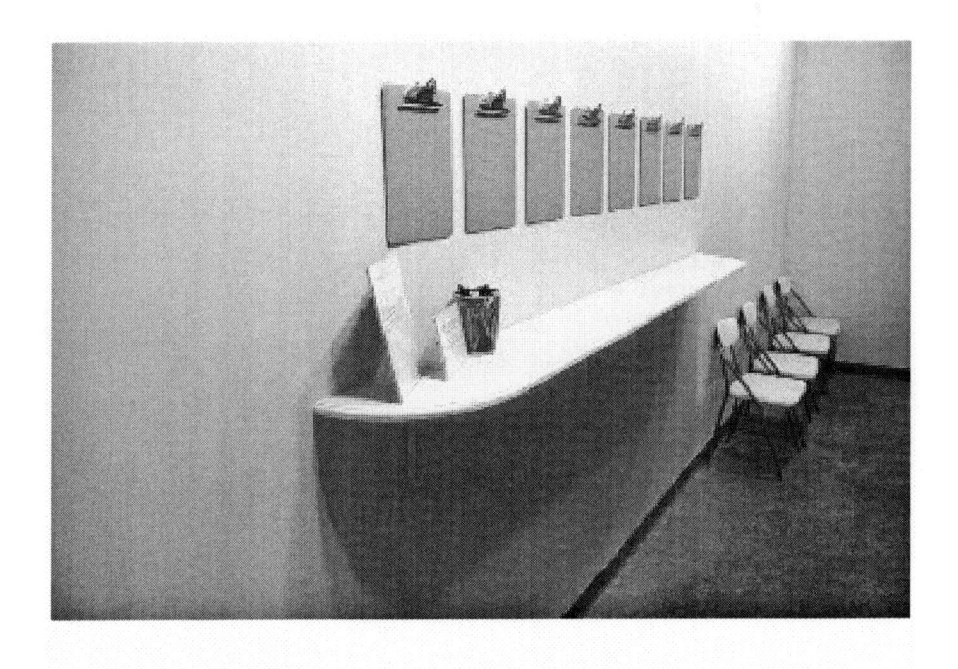

NOTE: *Monitor One* was trained by Patricia Rose and was required to interact with subjects in a manner that was in compliance with ISS research policies and provisions.

FLOOR PLAN

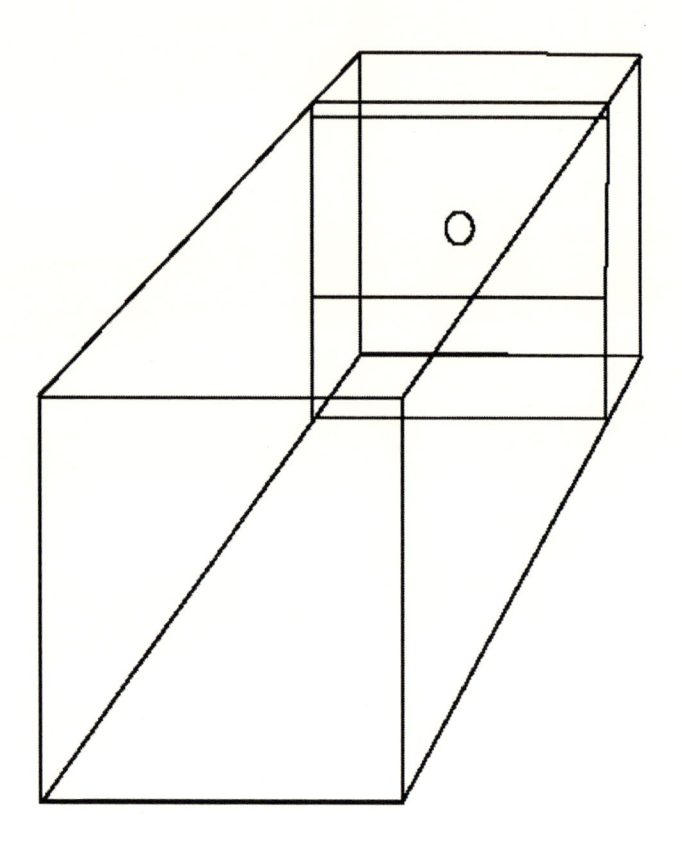

NOTE: The proportions of the testing site were established by ISS Researchers in collaboration with interior architects to create a spacious environment for subject interaction. The floor plan of the testing site is pertinent to the study, as space influenced subjects by establishing the parameters or proxemics for social exchange between the researcher and specimen.

TESTING

Patricia Rose (below) observed subjects within the testing site and verbally recited her observations in real time from behind the viewing window.

COMPARATIVE ANALYSIS

ID NUMBER	DATE OF BIRTH	SEX	IDEAL DIET/ HABITAT	SOCIABILITY Range: 1 (ANTISOCIAL) to 10 (GREGARIOUS)
05X563	12/11/1960	F	Organic/ Cocoon	10
07745	09/28/1955	M	Muffins/ Couch	3
027775	12/08/79	M	Soup/ Cold	5
099426	-/-/1988	M	Dirt/ Under Leaves	4
258399	04/10/54	M	Carnivore/ Water	3
368490	08/01/1975	F	Veg./ Near Water	2
583623	Subject form to be transcribed			1

NOTE: All categories listed above, with the exception of *Social Engagement*, were selfascribed classifications or identifiers, not attributed by the ISS or its affiliates. This small sampling from a study involving fifty-two subjects was chosen based on the self-identified gender and age of the specimens, as well as the level of sociability determined by ISS Researchers from observable data based upon the subjects' actions within the testing site.

SUBJECT SURVEY

SUBJECT IDENTIFICATION NUMBER: 05X563

PLEASE COMPLETE IN FULL AND RETURN TO THE MONITOR.

AGE: 50
WEIGHT: 140
HEIGHT: 5'5"
SEX: F
SPECIES: SLOVENIAN
IDEAL DIET AND HABITAT: ORGANIC — COCOON

LOCATION AND DATE OF BIRTH: MILWAUKEE — Dec. 11th

PLEASE LIST ANY PHYSICAL OR PSYCHOLOGICAL ABNORMALITIES THAT YOU HAVE:
Any and All

PLEASE LIST ANY CONTAGIOUS DISEASES THAT YOU ARE SUFFERING FROM:
Political Depression

PLEASE LIST EVERYTHING THAT YOU ARE ALLERGIC TO:
Republicans

DO YOU OR DOES ANYONE IN YOUR FAMILY SUFFER FROM DIABETES, HEART DISEASE, OR SYPHILIS? Y/N Maybe

THE INFORMATION THAT YOU HAVE PROVIDED WILL BE ASSESSED TO DETERMINE YOUR FITNESS BEFORE PARTICIPATION IN THE STUDY IS PERMITTED. BY SIGNING BELOW YOU ARE AGREEING TO PARTICIPATE IN THE STUDY AND ALL OF ITS COMPONENTS. YOU ARE ALSO ACKNOWLEDGING THAT THE ORGANIZERS WILL BE NOT HELD LIABLE FOR ANY COMPLICATIONS OR DAMAGES THAT MAY ARISE AS A RESULT OF THE EXPERIMENT.

SUBJECT SIGNATURE — DATE 9.22.10

SUBJECT ANALYSIS
IDENTIFICATION NUMBER: 05X563

MONITOR NOTES:

Immediate movement towards viewing window.

Quick to verbally engage with the monitor.

Signs of frustration evident in facial response.

Verbal Questioning: "What are your credentials?"

Continued social engagement, environmentally unconcerned.

Tendency towards analytical thought, expressed in verbal responses.

Continued emotional responses evident in facial expressions.

Exhibits little to no interest in the environment, solely interested in social engagement.

POST-EXPERIMENT SUMMARY:

Subject #05X563 was highly social and one of the few subjects within the experiment to voluntarily remain within the site once the door was unlocked by *Monitor One*.

SUBJECT SURVEY
SUBJECT IDENTIFICATION NUMBER: 007745
PLEASE COMPLETE IN FULL AND RETURN TO THE MONITOR.

AGE: 54
WEIGHT: 165
HEIGHT: 6'1"
SEX: M
SPECIES: Human
IDEAL DIET AND HABITAT: muffins and couch

LOCATION AND DATE OF BIRTH: St. Luke's Hospital 9/28/55

PLEASE LIST ANY PHYSICAL OR PSYCHOLOGICAL ABNORMALITIES THAT YOU HAVE:
NONE

PLEASE LIST ANY CONTAGIOUS DISEASES THAT YOU ARE SUFFERING FROM:
NONE

PLEASE LIST EVERYTHING THAT YOU ARE ALLERGIC TO:
some little things

DO YOU OR DOES ANYONE IN YOUR FAMILY SUFFER FROM DIABETES, HEART DISEASE, OR SYPHILIS? Y/N N

THE INFORMATION THAT YOU HAVE PROVIDED WILL BE ASSESSED TO DETERMINE YOUR FITNESS BEFORE PARTICIPATION IN THE STUDY IS PERMITTED. BY SIGNING BELOW YOU ARE AGREEING TO PARTICIPATE IN THE STUDY AND ALL OF ITS COMPONENTS. YOU ARE ALSO ACKNOWLEDGING THAT THE ORGANIZERS WILL BE NOT HELD LIABLE FOR ANY COMPLICATIONS OR DAMAGES THAT MAY ARISE AS A RESULT OF THE EXPERIMENT.

SUBJECT SIGNATURE   DATE 9/22/10

SUBJECT ANALYSIS
IDENTIFICATION NUMBER: 007745

MONITOR NOTES:

Slow to socialization.

Expresses signs of discomfort through facial twitches and laughing responses.

Quickly responds with curiosity to verbal prompts.

Relies primarily on non-verbal responses, despite a keen interest in the vocalizations of others demonstrated through body language.

Highly gestural expressions.

Environmental interest and awareness.

Passive responses to new environmental circumstances despite "humorous" or self-conscious behavior.

POST-EXPERIMENT SUMMARY:

Subject #007745 was slow to socialization until prompted by the vocalized observations of *Monitor One*. The subject approached the viewing window after a short time, however the subject rarely responded vocally and reacted primarily with gesticulations. The subject was environmentally and socially curious but mostly acted as a passive observer for the duration of the testing period.

SUBJECT SURVEY
SUBJECT IDENTIFICATION NUMBER: 099426
PLEASE COMPLETE IN FULL AND RETURN TO THE MONITOR.

AGE: 22
WEIGHT: 175
HEIGHT: 5'11"
SEX: ♀
SPECIES: Homo Sapien Sapien
IDEAL DIET AND HABITAT:
dirt   under leaves

LOCATION AND DATE OF BIRTH:
North   198

PLEASE LIST ANY PHYSICAL OR PSYCHOLOGICAL ABNORMALITIES THAT YOU HAVE:
Cat allergies

PLEASE LIST ANY CONTAGIOUS DISEASES THAT YOU ARE SUFFERING FROM:

PLEASE LIST EVERYTHING THAT YOU ARE ALLERGIC TO:
Cats
dogwood   golden rod
walnuts

DO YOU OR DOES ANYONE IN YOUR FAMILY SUFFER FROM DIABETES, HEART DISEASE, OR SYPHILIS? Y/(N)

THE INFORMATION THAT YOU HAVE PROVIDED WILL BE ASSESSED TO DETERMINE YOUR FITNESS BEFORE PARTICIPATION IN THE STUDY IS PERMITTED. BY SIGNING BELOW YOU ARE AGREEING TO PARTICIPATE IN THE STUDY AND ALL OF ITS COMPONENTS. YOU ARE ALSO ACKNOWLEDGING THAT THE ORGANIZERS WILL BE NOT HELD LIABLE FOR ANY COMPLICATIONS OR DAMAGES THAT MAY ARISE AS A RESULT OF THE EXPERIMENT.

SUBJECT SIGNATURE   DATE: 22/9/10

SUBJECT ANALYSIS
IDENTIFICATION NUMBER: 099426

MONITOR NOTES:

Slow to socialization.

Bodily discomfort and unease demonstrated in gesture or stance and physical distance from viewing window.

Self-conscious behavior evident in gesticulations.

Facial expressions indicate impatience.

Little to no vocalizations.

POST-EXPERIMENT SUMMARY:

Subject #099426 displayed signs of tension and physical unrest within the testing site. The subject appeared to be moderately anti-social, slowly advancing to the viewing window towards the end of the study period. #099426 was one of the most introverted subjects within the experiment.

SUBJECT SURVEY
SUBJECT IDENTIFICATION NUMBER: 258399
PLEASE COMPLETE IN FULL AND RETURN TO THE MONITOR.

AGE: 56
WEIGHT: 153 lbs.
HEIGHT: 5'9"
SEX: M
SPECIES: Humanoid
IDEAL DIET AND HABITAT:
Carnivore, Water.
LOCATION AND DATE OF BIRTH:
Milwaukee 4-10-54
PLEASE LIST ANY PHYSICAL OR PSYCHOLOGICAL ABNORMALITIES THAT YOU HAVE:
Abnormality compared to?

PLEASE LIST ANY CONTAGIOUS DISEASES THAT YOU ARE SUFFERING FROM:
Laughter

PLEASE LIST EVERYTHING THAT YOU ARE ALLERGIC TO:
Violence

DO YOU OR DOES ANYONE IN YOUR FAMILY SUFFER FROM DIABETES, HEART DISEASE, OR SYPHILIS? Y/N

THE INFORMATION THAT YOU HAVE PROVIDED WILL BE ASSESSED TO DETERMINE YOUR FITNESS BEFORE PARTICIPATION IN THE STUDY IS PERMITTED. BY SIGNING BELOW YOU ARE AGREEING TO PARTICIPATE IN THE STUDY AND ALL OF ITS COMPONENTS. YOU ARE ALSO ACKNOWLEDGING THAT THE ORGANIZERS WILL BE NOT HELD LIABLE FOR ANY COMPLICATIONS OR DAMAGES THAT MAY ARISE AS A RESULT OF THE EXPERIMENT.

SUBJECT SIGNATURE   DATE: 9-23-2010

SUBJECT ANALYSIS
IDENTIFICATION NUMBER: 258399

MONITOR NOTES:

Immediate movement towards the viewing window.

Quick to socialization and verbalization.

Little to no environmental interest.

Highly vocal subject with few extreme gesticulations or changes in stance.

Transition to non-verbal language through facial expressions.

Emotional responses are slight and hardly discernible.

Continued interest in socialization.

POST-EXPERIMENT SUMMARY:

Subject #258399 appeared to be socially curious and engaged but not easily readable. The subject responded through subtle facial expressions and short verbal comments.

SUBJECT SURVEY
SUBJECT IDENTIFICATION NUMBER: 586623
PLEASE COMPLETE IN FULL AND RETURN TO THE MONITOR.

AGE: 二十
WEIGHT: 五十四
HEIGHT: 一日口五 16.
SEX: 女 男
SPECIES: 人
IDEAL DIET AND HABITAT:
　　　白鱼
LOCATION AND DATE OF BIRTH:
　　　美国　　十一月一号
PLEASE LIST ANY PHYSICAL OR PSYCHOLOGICAL ABNORMALITIES THAT YOU HAVE:
　　　没有

PLEASE LIST ANY CONTAGIOUS DISEASES THAT YOU ARE SUFFERING FROM:
　　　没有

PLEASE LIST EVERYTHING THAT YOU ARE ALLERGIC TO:
　　　没有

DO YOU OR DOES ANYONE IN YOUR FAMILY SUFFER FROM DIABETES,
HEART DISEASE, OR SYPHILIS?   Y (N) 不

THE INFORMATION THAT YOU HAVE PROVIDED WILL BE ASSESSED TO DETERMINE YOUR FITNESS BEFORE
PARTICIPATION IN THE STUDY IS PERMITTED. BY SIGNING BELOW YOU ARE AGREEING TO PARTICIPATE
IN THE STUDY AND ALL OF ITS COMPONENTS. YOU ARE ALSO ACKNOWLEDGING THAT THE ORGANIZERS
WILL BE NOT HELD LIABLE FOR ANY COMPLICATIONS OR DAMAGES THAT MAY ARISE AS A RESULT OF THE
EXPERIMENT.

　　　　　　　　　　　　　　　　　　　　　　　　　九月二十二日
SUBJECT SIGNATURE　　　　　　　　　　　　　　　　DATE

SUBJECT ANALYSIS
IDENTIFICATION NUMBER: 586623

MONITOR NOTES:

Immediate movement towards the viewing window.

Displays an interest in vocal learning through repetition and mimicry.

Signs of confusion with Monitor's vocal observations.

Signs of impatience, demonstrated in facial expressions.

Environmentally uninterested.

Subject shows no signs of tension and appears calm throughout the testing process.

POST-EXPERIMENT SUMMARY:

Subject #586623 appeared to be socially interested but also passive. The subject did not aggressively engage in conversation and was one of the least reactive specimens in the experiment.

CONCLUSION

Post-test interviews were conducted with a sampling of subjects exactly one week after the testing process. One subject verbally recounted bouts of insomnia after participating in the experiment. When asked to elaborate, the subject explained that the testing process forced him to question his identity as a human being which was an "unsettling," introspective process. Other subjects made comments about feeling like "lab rats."

Some scientists would argue that the intention of an experiment is to collect, organize, and analyze data in order to find absolute truths or proof. The purpose of this experiment was to place subjects in a scenario where they were given reasonable control over the interaction in order to construct their own truths after being analyzed and subjected to an uncomfortable power dynamic.

By placing human subjects within a setting primarily reserved for "lab animals," subjects were forced to make choices which became both the data and the only discernible or objective truths derived from the experiment.

TESTING SITE II

ZOOSEMIOTIC TRANSLATION

EXPERIMENT DESCRIPTION

TESTING SITE II was created in order to gauge a subject's reaction to, or interpretation of, specific scientific visual examples. In this case, the visual prompts were abstractions of diagrammatic illustrations from zoosemiotic studies illustrating movement patterns of the *Honeybee Dance*.

Each visual prompt was structurally referential (i.e. linear and non-linear patterns, labels such as *'counter-structure'* or *'right left-movement,'* etc.). The following instructions were listed under each image for this online diagrammatic test: *Please study the diagram carefully and respond in any way that is applicable.* At the end of the study, subjects were required to complete a survey and classify themselves as *'adept'* or *'incompetent'* communicators without information detailing the form of communication or scale of competence in question.

Debates in the scientific community persist as to whether or not other animals communicate through systemized patterns. These debates cause ISS Researchers to question the human species' ability to interpret and decode representations of language patterns in other species of animals.

PRECEDENT

Sue Savage-Rumbaugh (1946—Present) was the first scientist to conduct research with bonobos, and has been studying the language capacity of apes since the 1970s. Savage-Rumbaugh has proposed that apes can not only mimic human language but can retain a variety of terms and corresponding gestures, interpret grammars, respond appropriately to context, and demonstrate the ability to invent language and new rules for usage that are comprehensible. Savage-Rumbaugh has been conducting research at the Great Ape Trust in Des Moines, Iowa, since 2005, using lexigrams or abstract symbols that are representative of words.

Other scientists and linguists have vehemently posited that the data derived from Savage-Rumbaugh's 'ape-language' studies is skewed or inaccurate. The reasons for these postulations are multi-fold, but the most cited examples have to do with the interactions between the researchers and apes. In his book *The Symbolic Species: The Co-Evolution of Language and the Brain*, Terrance W. Deacon questions the incentives in Savage-Rumbaugh's studies, the comprehension rates and anatomical limitations of apes, and also examines the definition of language itself, semioticially and symbolically.

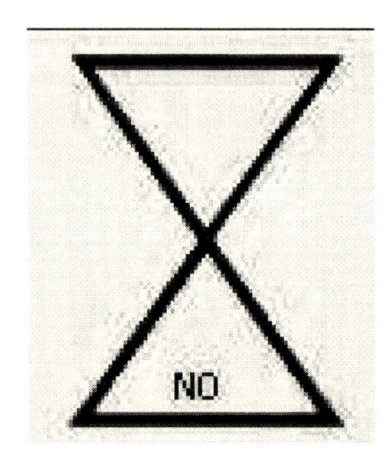

NOTE: This figure shows a lexigram that Savage-Rumbaugh installed on keyboards within the Great Ape Trust to study the lexical capacity of apes.

SELECTED DIAGRAMS

The following diagram is an abstraction of the *Honeybee Dance*, classified by semioticians as a zoosemiotic phenomenon. Subjects were prompted to interpret each active diagram online in order to gauge the level at which one cognizant species is able to interpret the communication patterns of another species.

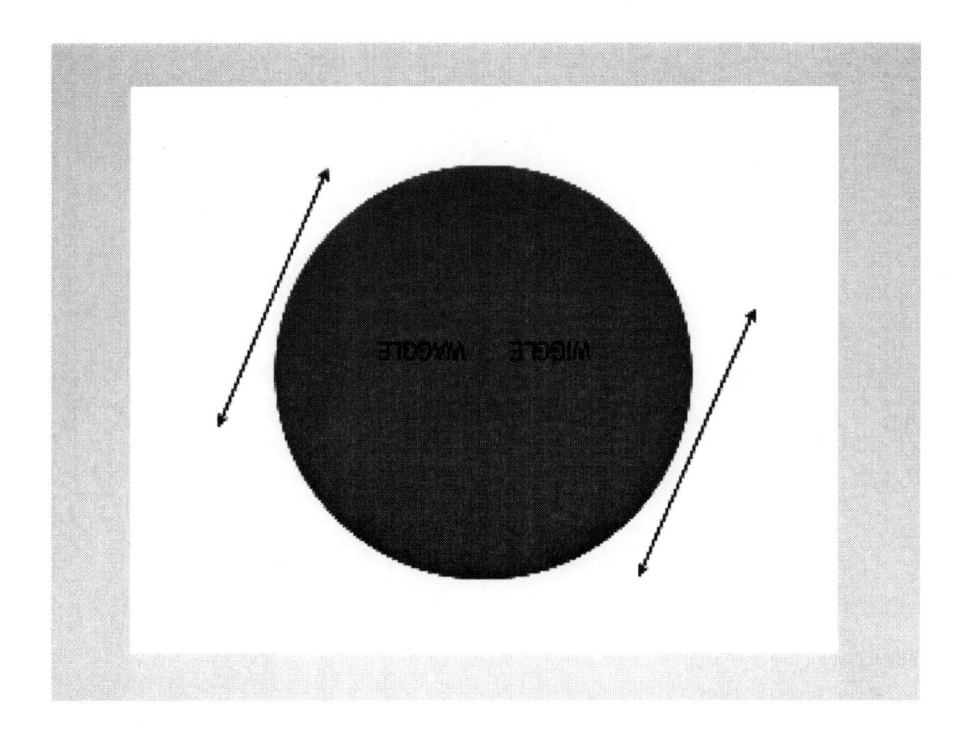

SELECTED DIAGRAMS

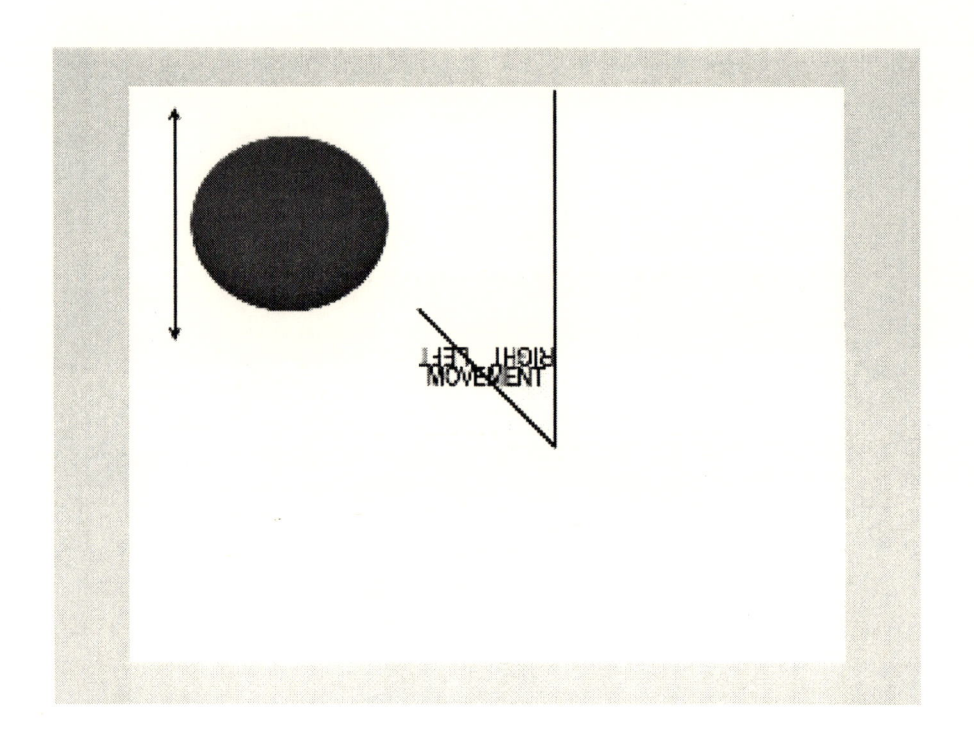

LEFT RIGHT
MOVEMENT

SELECTED DIAGRAMS

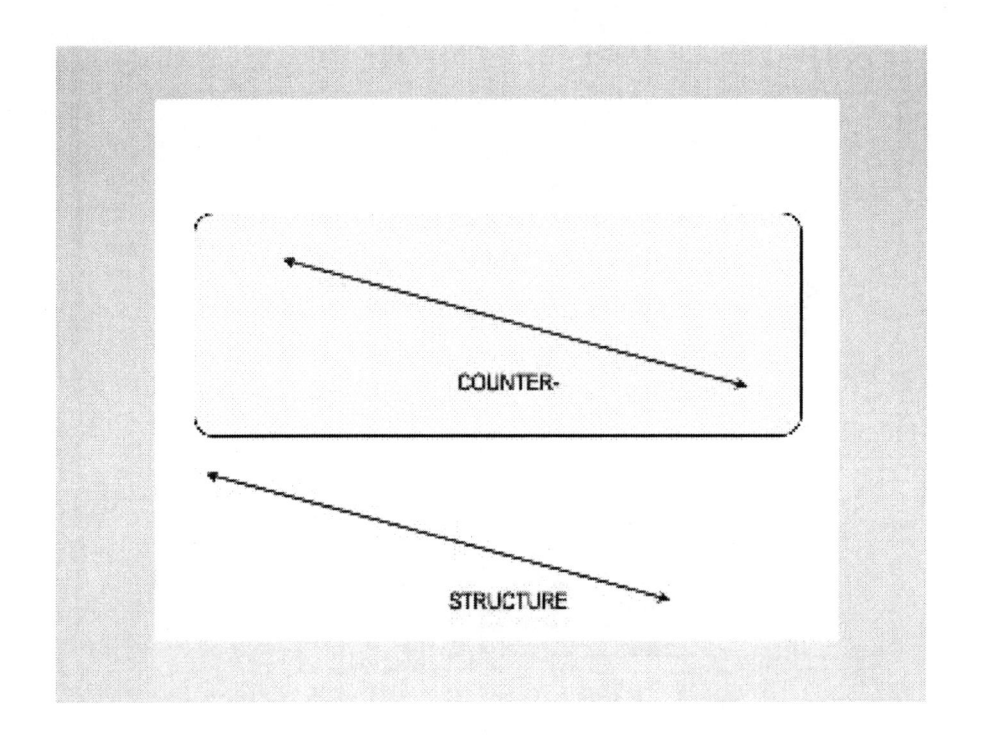

COUNTER-

STRUCTURE

COMPARATIVE ANALYSIS I

ID NUMBER	COMPLETION TIME	NUMBER OF RESPONSES	WORD COUNT OF LONGEST RESPONSE
0001	10:26 AM	4/4	103
0002	9:06 AM	4/4	37
0003	9:07 AM	4/4	42
0004	9:07 AM	4/4	41
0005	9:00 AM	4/4	12
0006	9:08 AM	4/4	34
0007	10:40 AM	4/4	1
0008	9:50 AM	4/4	14
0009	9:09 AM	4/4	28
0010	9:15 AM	4/4	23
0011	11:56 AM	4/4	1
0012	3:35 PM	4/4	60
0013	1:28 PM	4/4	25
0014	10:02 PM	4/4	6
0015	8:40 PM	4/4	4

NOTE: ISS Researchers were required to directly transcribe subject responses without interfering with the data. Correcting spelling, capitalization, punctuation, or any other grammatical errors was strictly prohibited by the Institute.

COMPARATIVE ANALYSIS II

1: How do you respond to the slides?

ID NUMBER	RESPONSE (FROM MULTIPLE CHOICE)	SUBJECT EXPLANATION (VOLUNTARY)
0001	Visually/Mentally	N/A
0002	Combination of Forms	N/A
0003	Gesturally/Combination of Forms	N/A
0004	Verbally	N/A
0005	Gesturally/Visually	N/A
0006	Visually	N/A
0007	Visually	N/A
0008	Gesturally/Visually	N/A
0009	Visually	N/A
0010	Verbally/Visually	N/A
0011	Visually	N/A
0012	Combination of Forms	I didn't respond to the slides per se as much as to the screens and to my expectations of what I found on the screens. I kept looking initially for some kind of movement based on the cursor, or something else to suddenly "pop up"—a Walker Percy "preformed symbolic complex" Also, the arrows and lines seems to invite play!

COMPARATIVE ANALYSIS II (cont.)

ID NUMBER	RESPONSE (FROM MULTIPLE CHOICE)	SUBJECT EXPLANATION (VOLUNTARY)
0013	Visually	N/A
0014	Combination of Forms	N/A
0015	Verbally/Visually/Gesturally/Combination of Forms	N/A

COMPARATIVE ANALYSIS III

2: Please interpret the forms within the experiment in the space provided below.

ID NUMBER	RESPONSE
0001	Certain words were used such as "direction" and "sign" for example along with arrows which together seem to lead me "some where." The block shapes or squares I read as roof tops or that I was being given the perspective of a birds eye view. This lead me to think I was looking at a map however the process I under went and the fact that I was given no destination and little instruction made me think I was being mapped or that I myself was mentally mapping things together in attempt to understand and that process in some way would be examined.
0002	there was a very minimal visual language consisting of text, line, and specific shapes. they were reminiscent of diagrams or primitive maps with arrows indicating a course of movement and lines and shapes indicating boundaries, areas, etc.
0003	I was confused. I expected that if I enacted the movements presented to me there would be some sort of response. Later, I thought maybe I was doing it wrong. I also didn't always understand what the prompt meant. I was impatient.
0004	They seemed to be about different types of movement... the diagrams served as ways to innocuously illustrate the words.
0005	geometric, lines, words, letters

COMPARATIVE ANALYSIS III (cont.)

ID NUMBER	SUBJECT RESPONSE
0006	Counter/structure was one particular test that stuck with me. I was unsure whether those two words where meant to be read together or separately. What is counter structure and why is that relevant
0007	lines
0008	The forms were generic and familiar, like inserts from Corel Paint or Windows Powerpoint.
0009	I found some of the forms to be understandable and interesting but some I had no idea what they were trying to convey.
0010	I felt that I needed some sort of context in which to place the diagrams for me to assign them any finite meaning.
0011	Dislocated
0012	By forms I think you mean the smaller windows, the lines, rays, points? To me, they read as "signs" — I felt comfortable decoding them, save the first one. That's a tough one!
0013	Symbols were present relating to movement, though actions were not definite/clear.
0014	lines, visuals
0015	tense

COMPARATIVE ANALYSIS IV

3: What examinations or thoughts did you have or make?

ID NUMBER	RESPONSE
0001	Confusion, disorientation
0002	i was constantly wanting to relate the text to the imagery, to force them to correspond, but not often able to make a strong connection between all presented information.
0003	I was confused. I expected that if I enacted the movements presented to me there would be some sort of response. Later, I thought maybe I was doing it wrong. I also didn't always understand what the prompt meant. I was impatient.
0004	The shapes are somewhat mind-numbing since everything is pretty much grey with text plus a little blue... I like the wiggle/waggle one though because it felt like it was doing just that because of how the text was positioned.
0005	i was trying to find a deeper meaning than maybe was necessary
0006	Counter-structure
0007	none
0008	I had little thought. Mostly reactions. Gestures.
0009	I found this to be really confusing. Especially at first, I kept trying to figure out if there was something else I was to do or just click on.
0010	Mostly it prompted me to think about the different forms of language in the experiment

COMPARATIVE ANALYSIS IV (cont.)

ID NUMBER	RESPONSE
0011	interesting
0012	I was struck by the clinical sparseness of the screens, and the lack of text. I found the screens to be inviting playgrounds, each a thought experiment. I did want to have an opportunity to respond somehow—I don't know how. I did think about speaking out a few times, expressing a frustration/whelp of delight.
0013	Geometry is universal. I see my teachers, dogs, and streets I grew up on.
0014	prepared for simple but difficult answers
0015	hesitation

COMPARATIVE ANALYSIS V

4: Do you consider yourself an adept communicator?

ID NUMBER	RESPONSE (FROM MULTIPLE CHOICE)	SUBJECT EXPLANATION (VOLUNTARY)
0001	No	I would say I am getting better.
0002	No	i am articulate, but i am not honest.
0003	No	medium bad/good communicator.
0004	Yes	I easily adopt accents and modes of speech of those I keep company with.
0005	Yes	N/A
0006	No	I do not understand
0007	No	N/A
0008	No	Thank you for having few questions.
0009	Yes	N/A
0010	No	N/A
0011	Yes	N/A
0012	N/A	Aha! Trick question!! No. There are far too many languages and dialects that I am deficient in. Also, I suppose I might ask, playfully, "What do you mean by the terms 'communicate', 'communicator,' and 'adept'? "Adept" meaning capable? Adequate? Functionally literate?

41

COMPARATIVE ANALYSIS V (cont.)

ID NUMBER	RESPONSE (FROM MULTIPLE CHOICE)	SUBJECT EXPLANATION (VOLUNTARY)
0013	No	adequate enough. I feel a constant pull between what is expected/how I'm supposed to react/societal expectations, and truth (especially in professional situations).
0014	Yes	depends on the situation
0015	No	N/A

CONCLUSION

The subjects who participated in this testing process were primarily college educated and between the ages of 19 and 56. Consequently, all subjects were institutionally conditioned and highly accustomed to testing formats and protocol. After a close analysis of data, it is apparent that ascribing the term *testing* to the process of inquiry induced anxiety in the subjects and influenced their responses. For example, in a post-test interview, a 20-year-old specimen expressed feelings of confusion in not having access to the *right answer*.

More than half of the subjects verbally expressed signs of confusion. Subjects indicated frustration when they were unable to decode patterns, particularly when the patterns appeared to have discernible content that was difficult to access and interpret. The instructions were not explicit and subjects struggled with a testing format that allowed the opportunity of choice.

In short, the experiment failed. The only discernible conclusion formulated by ISS Researchers was that most human specimens are unable to decode abstractions of the *Honeybee Dance* without a preprescribed diagrammatic label. Although humans invented the structure of testing formats, many are too institutionally conditioned to break beyond an established structure during the testing process or to feel comfortable responding candidly.

TESTING SITE III

SPECIES-CENTRIC WORD ASSOCIATION

EXPERIMENT DESCRIPTION

TESTING SITE III was created to examine a subject's response to textual and situational variables simultaneously and to examine the human species' translation of species-centric terms.

Subjects were required to complete a *Subject Survey* in which they were asked to classify themselves as a part of the human species, explicate their preferred method of communication, and list other relevant taxonomic characteristics or personality traits.

In this experiment, subjects were required to examine a list of words and respond by writing down the term that they thought most appropriately corresponded with the provided term on the list. Examining terms based on their ascribed meaning and on the basis of their co-occurence with other terms is one essential component of a word association test.

Inspired by the ideas of Sir Francis Galton, TESTING SITE III was staged within an art exhibition. Subjects were on display as they completed individual tests with associative components. Thus, contextual relationships between the subject, audience, and individual terms were all of vital importance to both their response and this study.

PRECEDENT

Sir Francis Galton (1822—1911) was a scientist committed to the study of human intelligence. Galton created the first word association or personality tests as well as the concept of eugenics, all of which were influenced by data derived from his installation of the *Anthropometric Lab*, in the 1884 World's Fair in London.

In Larry H. Ludlow's article "Galton: The First Psychometrician?," Galton was cited as having said that, "... until the phenomena of any branch of knowledge has been subjected to measurement and numbers, it cannot assume the status and dignity of a science."

ANTHROPOMETRIC LABORATORY
For the measurement in various ways of Human Form and Faculty.
Entered from the Science Collection of the S. Kensington Museum.

This laboratory is established by Mr. Francis Galton for the following purposes:-

1. For the use of those who desire to be accurately measured in many ways, either to obtain timely warning of remediable faults in development, or to learn their powers.
2. For keeping a methodological register of the principal measurements of each person, of which he may at any future time obtain a copy under reasonable restrictions. His initials and date of birth will be entered in the register, but not his name. The names are indexed in a separate book.
3. For supplying information on the methods, practice, and uses of human measurement.
4. For anthropometric experiment and research, and for obtaining data for statistical discussion.

Charges for the making of principal measurements:
THREEPENCE each, to those who are already on the Register.
FOURPENCE eac, to those who are not:- one page of the Register will thenceforward be assigned to them, and a few extra measurements will be made chiefly for future identification.

The Superintendent is charged with the control of the laboratory and with determining in each case, which, if any, of the extra measurements may be made and under what conditions.

H. & W. Brown, Printers, 20 Fulham Road, S.W.

TESTING SITE

Subjects were required to sit at the desk for the duration of the testing process.

NOTE: The color of the testing site was a bright, light sea-blue-green. The color is relevant, as it influenced the tonality of the space and interactions between subjects and the audience.

COMPARATIVE ANALYSIS I

TOTAL # OF SUBJECTS	11
TOTAL # OF MALE SUBJECTS	5
TOTAL # OF FEMALE SUBJECTS	5
TOTAL # OF GENDERLESS SUBJECTS	1
WEIGHT RANGE	133—186
MOST COMMON SELF-ASCRIBED SPECIES	HUMAN/HOMO SAPIEN
YEAR OF BIRTH RANGE	1956—1993
HANDWRITING: PRINT	9
HANDWRITING: SCRIPT	2
RESPONDED YES TO ACA (ADEPT COMMUNICATION ASSESSMENT)	6
RESPONDED NO TO IAC (INEPT COMMUNICATION)	3
RESPONDED INCONCLUSIVE AC (ADEPT COMMUNICATOR)	2
TOTAL # OF SUBJECTS LISTING ABNORMALITIES	10
TOTAL # OF SUBJECT WITH OFFSPRING	0
TOTAL # OF SUBJECTS THAT SIGNED CONSENT	10

SUBJECT SURVEY

IDENTIFICATION NUMBER: 340

WEIGHT: 135

SEX: F

SPECIES: human

IDEAL DIET & HABITAT: pasta   a big grassy field

LOCATION AND DATE OF BIRTH: Oconomowoc, WI
11/21/91

NUMBER OF OFFSPRING: 0

PHYSICAL OR PSYCHOLOGICAL ABNORMALITIES:

larger right ankle and big red hair

DO YOU CONSIDER YOURSELF TO BE AN ADEPT COMMUNICATOR?

no

WHAT FORM OF COMMUNICATION DO YOU RELY UPON MOST HEAVILY?

noises

HOW DO YOU INTERACT WITH OTHERS?

laughing at whatever they say

BY SIGNING BELOW YOU ARE AGREEING TO PARTICIPATE IN THE STUDY AND ALL OF ITS COMPONENTS. YOU ARE WILLINGLY RELEASING THE INFORMATION THAT YOU PROVIDE TO THE INSTITUTE FOR SPECIES SYSTEMIZATION FOR ANALYSIS. YOU ARE ALSO ACKNOWLEDGING THAT THE ORGANIZERS WILL BE NOT HELD LIABLE FOR ANY COMPLICATIONS OR DAMAGES THAT MAY ARISE AS A RESULT OF THE EXPERIMENT.

SIGNATURE   11/12/10
                                            DATE

1. CAREFULLY EXAMINE THE TERMS LISTED BELOW. 340
2. PLEASE WRITE ONE WORD ACROSS FROM EACH TERM.

SUBJECT	MATTER	VASE	GLASS
TAPE	RECORDER	THREATENED	OUTSIDE
ANOTHER	PERSON	BLUE	TEAL
HUMAN	SKIN	LANGUAGE	MOVEMENT
LOGICAL	PARANOID	CONCLUSIONS	INTRODUCTIONS
SWEATER	LAMB	ZOOSEMIOTICS	STUPID
TAXONOMY	SHOPPING	YELLOW	GREEN
PRIMAL	MATING	CLASSIFICATIONS	MOTHER
PERCEPTUAL	POWER	EMPATHY	SORRY
ETHICAL	STUDIES	PUNCTUATION	!
SOCIAL	ISSUES	IMPLICATIONS	WHY
CANDID	LAUGHTER	DEDUCTION	NEGATIVE
MECHANISTIC	FATHER	OBJECTS	WALLS
CONTAINED	BOX	CLARITY	CONFUSING
SPECIES	PLANTS	SYSTEM	SYMBOL
MANUFACTURED	FACTORY	VOCABULARIES	CHARLIE
LEARNED	ABSORB	ASSUMPTIONS	INTRODUCTION
ANTHROPOMORPHIC	OKAY	MISUNDERSTANDING	ALWAYS
PRECARIOUS	CAT	PRONOUNS	GRAMMER
OVERT	SHIT	INFERENCES	SOCCER
SUBTLE	WHISPERS	SLURS	DRUNK
HAPPY	BIRTHDAY	HIERARCHY	PERCEPTION

COMPARATIVE ANALYSIS II

1: What form of communication do you rely upon most heavily?

ID NUMBER	RESPONSE
330	Blabbing
331	Words
339	Speaking, Writing, Art-Making
336	Telephone
340	Noises
332	The sensation of touch
341	Physically vocal abstraction
329	Talking in person
335	Writing and Speaking
338	Vocal
337	I speak with my body

COMPARATIVE ANALYSIS III

2: How do you interact with others?

ID NUMBER	RESPONSE
330	All sorts of ways!
331	Sometimes not at all. I regard others as potential.
339	Speaking, Writing, Art-Making
336	Talking
340	Laughing at whatever they say
332	Touching and laughing, intimate interaction
341	Aggressively tactile frontal engagement
329	Politely and then casually
335	Speaking, Looking, Yes and No, Listening
338	I like to observe people during forms of communication
337	Signatures and handshakes

COMPARATIVE ANALYSIS IV

3: Ideal Diet & Habitat

ID NUMBER	RESPONSE
330	Eating Noodles in a Yurt
331	Natural, balanced. Urban jungles
339	Comfy warm home in metropolitan city. Pasta, meats and cheese
336	Raw fish/close to water
340	Pasta, a big grassy field
332	Candy Bakery Fruits
341	Clear water and intent
329	Nutritious and safe
335	Healthy, mostly veg.
338	Beer, grilled seafood on the coast
337	People, Dreams.

COMPARATIVE ANALYSIS V

4: Physical or Psychological Abnormalities

ID NUMBER	RESPONSE
330	lazy eyes, weird hands, and a butt chin
331	I have large feet and slightly broad shoulders. I am ticklish on my back. I am skeptical. I can wiggle my ears and flip my eyelids. I am inspired. Personality in itself is an abnormality, isn't it? I question a lot of things.
339	Slightly overanalyzing, a workaholic, sometimes left leg shorter than right, nearsighted
336	onset OCD
340	larger right ankle and big red hair
332	produce too many skin cells on scalp talk to self and fantasize the world as it should or should not be, rather than how it is
341	fluffly yet dense upon progressive contact
329	allergic to cephzil metal in hand
335	bi-polar
338	a needed desire to take tests
337	Normality = Abnormality. It's a vicious cycle.

COMPARATIVE ANALYSIS (WORD ASSOCIATIONS)

ID NUMBER	TERMS			
	SUBJECT	VASE	TAPE	THREATENED
330	MATTER	SCENARIO	BALL	N/A
331	ANSWER	EARTH	HOLD	PUSH
339	OBJECT	TULIP	RECORDER	ENDANGERED
336	MATTER	PASE	DUCT	DEER
340	MATTER	GLASS	RECORDER	OUTSIDE
332	ZOO	POT	RECORDER	RETALIATE
341	TIME	CHASM	BOUND	TIGHTEN
329	NOUN	UGLY	DECK	DARFUR
335	OBJECT	FLOWER	RULER	RUN
338	THIS TEST	DECORATION	STICK	VIOLATE
337	VASE	VASE	/////////////////////	/////////////////////
ID NUMBER	ANOTHER	BLUE	HUMAN	LANGUAGE
330	ONE	POOP	HEAD	SLANG
331	SYSTEMATIC	STILLNESS	TEMPORARY	CAMERA
339	MAN	TEAL	MIND	BILINGUAL
336	ONE	MOON	-OID	CROATION
340	PERSON	TEAL	SKIN	MOVEMENT
332	RECORD	DEDUBADIC	GENOME	ENGLISH
341	GIRL	CAR	FLESH	ORDINARY
329	FRIEND	NEBULA	BEING	DENTSCHE
335	SAME	SKY	ANIMAL	WORD
338	ALTERNATIVE	CALM	ANIMAL	COMMUNICA-TION
337	HOTDOG	HMBGR	N/A	N/A

COMPARATIVE ANALYSIS (WORD ASSOCIATIONS)

ID NUMBER	LOGICAL	CONCLUSIONS	SWEATER	ZOOSEMIOTICS
330	ANSWER	JUMP	VEST	COSMETOLOGY
331	INCONCLUSIVE	MEANING	KNIT	WHAT
339	BRAIN	ANSWERS	KNIT	DICTIONARY
336	REASON	STORY	VEST	N/A
340	PARANOID	INTRODUCTIONS	LAMB	STUPID
332	RESPONSE	ANSWERS	VEST	QUASIPHYSICS
341	MONKEY	FUTILE	LEATHER	ZOO
329	STATEMENT	DETERMINE	WARM	COSMOS
335	PRACTICAL	DRAW	COAT	ZOOS
338	ANALYTICAL	ENDINGS	WARM	COOL WORD
337	N/A	N/A	N/A	N/A

ID NUMBER	TAXONOMY	YELLOW	PRIMAL	CLASSIFICATIONS
330	WHAAAT?	JACKET	INSTINCT	SHMLASSIFICATIONS
331	MURDER	BURN	LASH	GENERAL
339	BIRDS	BIRD	INSTINCT	SCIENCE
336	ANIMAL	BEE	INSTINCT	N/A
340	SHOPPING	GREEN	MATING	MOTHER
332	TAXATION	SUBMARINE	INSTINCT	LIBRARY
341	FELINE	SKIN	HAIR	1989
329	YMONOXAT	QUASAR	INSTINCT	NAZI
335	DEAD	COLOR	SCREAM	TERM
338	N/A	HEATING UP	CORE	LISTS
337	N/A	N/A	N/A	N/A

58

COMPARATIVE ANALYSIS (WORD ASSOCIATIONS)

ID NUMBER	PERCEPTUAL	EMPATHY	ETHICAL	PUNCTUATION
330	INTELLECTUAL	SHMEMPATHY	TREATMENT	SHMUNCTUATION
331	BEAUTIFUL	FEEL	INSTANTANEOUS	HELP
339	SIGHT	SYMPATHY	MIND SET	MARK
336	VISION	FUNERAL	BS	N/A
340	POWER	SORRY	STUDIES	!
332	CONVOLUTED	EXSTACY	QUANDARY	EXCLAMATION
341	CROSS EYED	SMILE	BLACK	DOT
329	BLISS	BABIES	NON-ETHICAL	PERIOD
335	OBSERVE	SAD	SIN	EMPHASIS
338	VISION	REGARD	THOUGHTFUL	COMPLETION
337	N/A	N/A	N/A	N/A
ID NUMBER	SOCIAL	IMPLICATIONS	CANDID	DEDUCTION
330	NETWORK	SHMIMPLICATIONS	CAMERA	SHMDEDUCTION
331	OBLIGATORY	MANIPULATIVE	FALSE	ANSWER
339	BACKGROUND	CRIME	PHOTOGRAPH	CRIME
336	UNDERSTAND	SOCIAL	CAMERA	DEDUCE
340	ISSUES	WHY	LAUGHTER	NEGATIVE
332	INTERACTION	INVITATION	CAMERA	REASONING
341	WORKER	TEETH	CANDY	(-)
329	EXPERIMENT	JUDGE	CAMERA	LOSS
335	ALONE	EFFECT	FUN	REALIZE
338	TALKATIVE	HINTS	OPEN	DISCOVERY
337	N/A	N/A	N/A	N/A

COMPARATIVE ANALYSIS (WORD ASSOCIATIONS)

ID NUMBER	MECHANISTIC	OBJECTS	CONTAINED	CLARITY
330	TURD	SHMOBJECTS	TUPPERWARE	SHMLARITY
331	PURPOSE	UNKNOWN	RESTRAINED	GHOSTS
339	ROBOT	OFFICE	PRESERVED	TRANSPARENT
336	HAMMER	GLASS	TUPPERWARE	N/A
340	FATHER	WALLS	BOX	CONFUSING
332	MECHANISM	ART	ECOSYSTEM	VISION
341	MASOCHISTIC	MIASMIC	JAR	EYE
329	PENIS	EXCITING	FORM	FREEDOM
335	RIGID	SOLIDS	SPACE	SEE
338	PROCEDURE	THINGS	HELD	UNDERSTAND
337	N/A	N/A	N/A	N/A

ID NUMBER	SPECIES	SYSTEM	MANUFACTURED	VOCABULARIES
330	FLEECIES	SHMYSTEM	CHEESE	SCHOCABULARIES
331	DISSECTION	SYTAX	ORDINARY	DOUBLE
339	ANIMAL	REQUIREMENTS	CAR	TIME
336	ORIGIN	OVERLOAD	CHEESE	SHORTENED
340	PLANTS	SYMBOLS	FACTORY	CHARLIE
332	ALIEN	COMPUTERS	HAPPINESS	LANGUAGES
341	LINGUAL	EXACT	BRILLO	MINUTE
329	PART II	FAILED	SILICON	LACK
335	HUMAN	CLASS	CREATE	WORDS
338	HUMAN	SOLAR	MADE UP	N/A
337	N/A	N/A	N/A	N/A

COMPARATIVE ANALYSIS (WORD ASSOCIATIONS)

ID NUMBER	LEARNED	ASSUMPTIONS	ANTHROPO-MORPHIC	MISUNDER-STANDING
330	SHELLY LEARNED	SHMASSUMP-TIONS	APE	SHMISUNDER-STANDING
331	PERSEVERE	KILL	LONG	LIE
339	LOVE	WRONG	LANDSCAPE	COMMON
336	CUSTOM	N/A	ETHNOMOR-PHIC	N/A
340	ABSORB	INTRODUCTION	OKAY	ALWAYS
332	INSTINCT	WRONG	FURRY	RIGHT
341	CHALK	BIRTHDAY	RUBBER	CHEAT
329	TO SPELL	STEREOTYPE	STUDIES	AWKWARD
335	CREATIVE	RASH	ESSENCE	COMMUNICATE
338	DISCOVERED	GUESSING	CHANGING	DO TO ASSUMPTIONS
337	N/A	N/A	N/A	N/A
ID NUMBER	**PRECARIOUS**	**PRONOUNS**	**OVERT**	**INFERENCES**
330	CLIFF	SHMNOUNS	INDIVIDUAL	SHMINFER-ENCES
331	CAREFUL	SPECIAL	PLANE	LOOK
339	PITCHER	VERBS	STYLE	PROCESS
336	GIRL	N/A	EGS	N/A
340	CAT	GRAMMAR	SHIT	SOCCER
332	EDGE	ME	SUBSTANCE	YOU
341	DRIP	NONE	AVERT	GLOW
329	CAT	SHE	OPERATION	INDRA
335	FREE	SUBJECT	EXTRA	INFLUENCED
338	THRILL	N/A	LOUD	N/A
337	N/A	N/A	N/A	N/A

COMPARATIVE ANALYSIS (WORD ASSOCIATIONS)

ID NUMBER	SUBTLE	SLURS	HAPPY	HIERARCHY
330	SCUTTLE	SHMLURS	CLAM	SHMERARCHY
331	CRYING	DENOUNCE	THROBBING	LORD
339	TENDENCIES	DRUNK	MOMENT	POPE
336	BEARD	EBONICS	DUCK	NONE
340	WHISPERS	DRUNK	BIRTHDAY	PERCEPTION
332	SEXY	BLACKS	BIRTHDAY	AWESOME
341	DESERT	PUDDLE	NOT	PANOPTICON
329	SARCASM	SLANG	BIRTHDAY	MAFIA
335	SUBLIMINAL	ACCIDENTS	SAD	PYRAMID
338	QUIET	SLOPPY	SMILE	ORDER
337	N/A	N/A	N/A	N/A

CONCLUSION

Eleven subjects were tested, resulting in a broad range of answers. Subjects #335 and #338 demonstrated similar thought processes based upon the frequency of concordant lexical responses. Subjects #330 and #337 chose not to complete the test in full and were either unresponsive to over 50% of the testing materials or repeated the preprescribed term with added syllables.

As a result of the format of this psycholinguistic study, subjects chose not to acknowledge the patterns between the selected species-centric terminology. Thus, the associative rules that typically apply in such studies were not demonstrated by this sampling of subjects. For example, on the testing materials the following terms were listed parallel, in order to test the ability of these specimens to recognize meaningful patterns disguised within a structure.

ETHICAL	PUNCTUATION
SOCIAL	IMPLICATIONS
SPECIES	SYSTEM
MANUFACTURED	VOCABULARIES
LEARNED	ASSUMPTIONS
ANTHROPOMORPHIC	MISUNDERSTANDING
PRECARIOUS	PRONOUNS
OVERT	INFERENCES
SUBTLE	SLURS
HAPPY	HIERARCHY

In this case, subjects did not seem to fully recognize the implications of their linguistic choices, evident in the racist responses for the term SLURS.

TESTING SITE IV

PSYCHOLINGUISTIC PERCEPTUAL STUDY

EXPERIMENT DESCRIPTION

TESTING SITE IV was created in order to allow participants to embody a role within a clear hierarchical scenario and engage actively in species-centric inquiry with another subject.

Subjects were required to complete a *Subject Survey* in which they classified themselves as a part of the human species, explicated their preferred method of communication, and listed other taxonomic characteristics or personality traits. *Monitors* (in this case drawn from the pool of participants) were required to review the informed consent materials and the monitor protocol established by the ISS.

Participants assigned the role of *Monitor* were instructed to: A) determine whether the specimen or subject was a cognizant sentient being, B) record seven behavioral responses, and C) record vocalized subject responses as part of a two page questionnaire.

Social interactions were influenced by the proxemics established in the trapezoidal space as well as the barrier established by the viewing window, but ultimately participants were in control of the interactions that took place within the testing site. This experiment was structured with the assumption that the human species will obey or comply with the rules of an organizer, without completely understanding the outcome or implications of their chosen compliance.

PRECEDENT

Adelbert Ames Jr. (1880—1955) was a scientist who conducted perceptual studies. His most noteworthy experiment, the *Ames Room*, was built in 1946 and was composed of an inclined floor and trapezoidal walls which shifted the viewers' understanding of space. Although the floor appeared level and the space appeared cubic, it was a perceptual trick that affected the scale of subjects or objects within a structure.

Ames was also an ophthalmologist, and he developed a cure for the disorder that he named "Aniseikonia," which is Greek for *unequal images*.

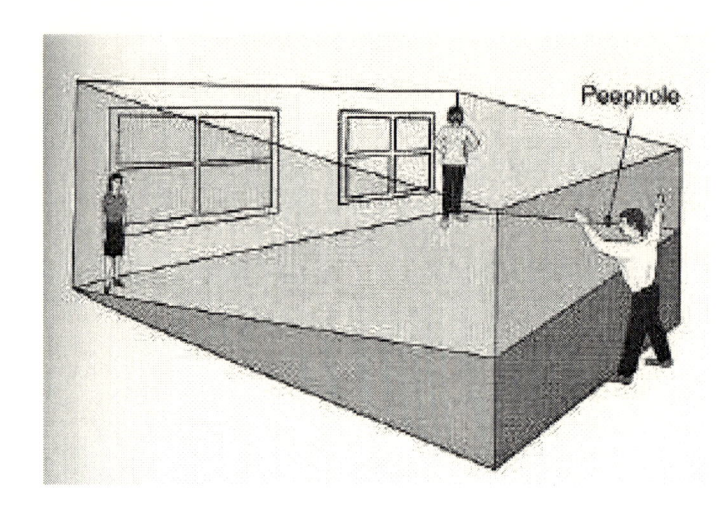

TEST PROTOCOLS & PROCEDURES

SUBJECT PROTOCOL AND PROCEDURES

Thank you for taking the time to participate. Your participation enables the ISS to continue our studies.

YOUR COMPLIANCE IS REQUIRED FOR THE SUCCESS OF THIS STUDY.

PLEASE FOLLOW THE INSTRUCTIONS DICTATED BY THE MONITOR.

YOU ARE REQUIRED TO RESPOND TO THE MONITOR'S PROMPTS.

0037/S

INFORMED CONSENT

MONITOR PROTOCOL AND PROCEDURES

Thank you for taking the time to participate. Your participation enables the ISS to continue our studies.

YOUR TASK AS A MONITOR IS TO VISUALLY EXAMINE THE BEHAVIORS OF A SUBJECT AND ACCURATELY RECORD ALL OBSERVABLE DATA OR SUBJECT RESPONSES (GESTURAL, VERBAL, BEHAVIORAL, ETC.)

MAINTAIN A LEVEL OF PROFESSIONALISM WHEN CONDUCTING THESE STUDIES. FOLLOW ALL INSTRUCTIONS WITHIN THE TESTING PACKET.

IT IS CRITICAL THAT YOU MAINTAIN A LEVEL OF OBJECTIVITY. DO NOT VERBALLY OR GESTURALLY ACKNOWLEDGE THE SPECIMEN'S REACTIONS. IF THE SUBJECT POSES ANY QUESTIONS ABOUT THE STUDY, PLEASE SAY: *"SUBJECT PARTICIPATION IS VOLUNTARY"* OR *"WE ARE NOT AT LIBERTY TO DISCLOSE INFORMATION ABOUT THE STUDY AT THIS TIME."*

IF THE TESTING PROCESS EXCEEDS TEN MINUTES, YOUR STUDY WILL BE INTERRUPTED. YOU WILL BE ASKED TO TERMINATE THE STUDY AND LEAVE THE TESTING SITE. THE SUBJECT WILL BE RELEASED.

0037/M

RECEPTION

Participants were received by a *Monitor* who instructed them to complete a *Subject Survey*, or review the *Informed Consent* paperwork, depending on the assigned role.

TESTING

After the proper paperwork was completed, *Subjects* and *Monitors* were locked into the testing site (below).

FLOOR PLAN (TOP VIEW)

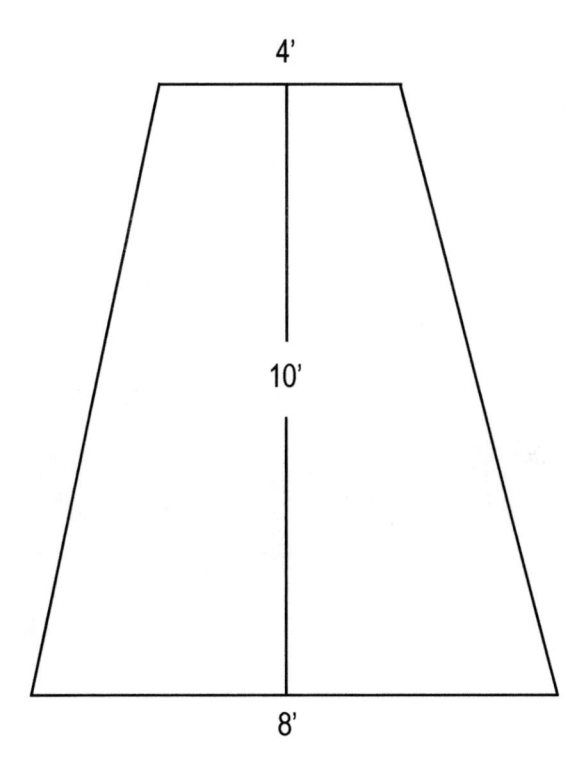

4'

10'

8'

NOTE: The floor plan of the testing site is pertinent to this study, as space was one of the factors that influenced subjects by establishing the parameters for social exchange between participants.

TESTING

Subjects were observed within the testing site through a surveillance camera (a frame of which may be seen below) to ensure that all participants were acting in accordance with the parameters of the experiment and following the proper protocol established by the ISS.

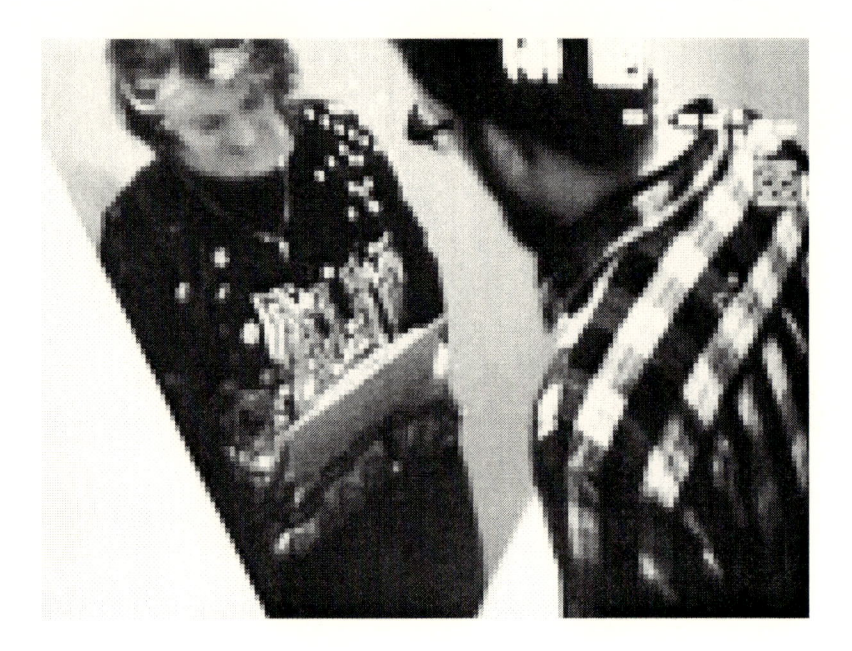

TESTING

After the participant who acted as the *Monitor* observed the *Subject* and completed the testing materials in full, Patricia Rose released both participants from the enclosure.

NOTE: Those who embodied the role of *Monitor* were asked to strive for objectivity while recording the subject's behavioral or lexical responses.

COMPARATIVE ANALYSIS I

TOTAL # OF SUBJECTS (INCLUDES *SUBJECTS* AND *MONITORS*)	64
TOTAL # OF MALE SUBJECTS (UNLESS OTHERWISE SPECIFIED, NUMBERS ONLY INCLUDE *SUBJECT* RESPONSES)	19
TOTAL # OF FEMALE SUBJECTS	10
TOTAL # OF GENDERLESS SUBJECTS	2
WEIGHT RANGE	69—278
YEAR OF BIRTH RANGE	1950—1998
TOTAL # OF *SUBJECTS* LISTING ABNORMALITIES	16
TOTAL # OF *SUBJECTS* WITH OFFSPRING	7
TOTAL # OF *SUBJECTS* THAT SIGNED CONSENT * (INCLUDES BOTH *SUBJECTS* AND *MONITORS*)	64

COMPARATIVE ANALYSIS II

17: What distinguishing factors separate you from other animals?

ID NUMBER	RESPONSE
168	None more so than any other animals from each other. Humans are more agressive usually.
174	Thumbs, Brains
178	BI PEDAL
204	Ability to form tools, create art, communicate on a higher level
207	Um...hm...I would say the only thing would be a larger frontal lobe...linked to higher logic. But I don't know what a squirrel thinks about right or wrong so I can't say.
449	...creativity
457	I don't know how to answer that.
467	no difference in kind, only in degree
469	thinking
471	I am human and I stand on two legs and I have a bigger brain, intellect, emotion etc.
465	my height
463	critical thinking
461	height, weight, facial features
455	Lack of hair
182	physical, behavioral language

CONCLUSION

TESTING SITE IV produced the most scattered data set of any experiment conducted by the ISS thus far. Half of the subjects were assigned the role of *Monitor* and required to record vocal and behavioral responses of other *Subjects*. This experimental method produced dynamic but unquantifiable results.

Approximately fifteen subjects struggled with the questions, whereas ten subjects appeared to answer with certainty the questions that were formulated and sequenced by the ISS based on the level of percieved difficulty.

TESTING SITE IV produced little data suitable for a general analysis. The study is only successful in that it highlighted the difficulty of reaching absolute conclusions when prompting psycholingustic species-centric inquiry.

BIBLIOGRAPHY

Galton, Francis. "Hereditary Genius: An Inquiry into Its Laws and Consequences." *Sir Francis Galton F.R.S: 1822-1911.* 1892. Web. 17 Nov. 2010. <http://galton.org/>.

Great Ape Trust. *Bonobos, Orangutans and the Study of Ape Language, Tools and Intelligence.* Web. 18 June 2011. <http://www.greatapetrust.org/>.

Harlow, Harry. "The Nature of Love." *American Psychologist.* Vol. 13 (1958): 673-85. *Classics in the History of Psychology.* Christopher D. Green, Mar. 2000. Web. 18 June 2011. <http://psychclassics.yorku.ca/Harlow/love.htm?session=0JhSMuyOISMG0UXiTCTJCtKVtF>.

Implicit Association Test. Harvard University, 1998. Web. 17 Nov. 2010. <http://implicit.harvard.edu/>.

"Medicine: Aniseikonia." Editorial. *Time Magazine* 30 Apr. 1934. Web. 18 June 2011. <http://www.time.com/time/magazine/article/0,9171,930496,00.html>.

Noth, Winfried. *The Handbook of Semiotics.* Sept. 28, 1995, Indiana U.P. Pinker, Steven. The Language Instinct. Sept. 4 2007, Harper.

Pinker, Steven. *The Language Instinct.* New York: W. Morrow, 1994. Print.

Shennan, Stephen. *Pattern and Process in Cultural Evolution: Origins of Human Behavior and Culture.* March 31, 2009, U.P. California.

Sir Francis Galton. *Gavan Tredoux.* Web. 18 June 2011. <http://galton.org/>.

W. Deacon, Terrence. *The Symbolic Species: The Co-Evolution of Language and the Brain.* April 1998, W. W. Norton & Co.

Waal, Frans De. *Primates and Philosophers: How Morality Evolved.* Ed. Stephen Macedo and Josiah Ober. 1st ed. New Jersey: Princeton UP, 2006. Print.

Wiers, Reinout W., and Alan W. Stacy, eds. *Handbook of Implicit Cognition and Addiction.* Vol. 1. Sage Publications, 2005. Print.

BIOGRAPHY

Patricia Rose is a leading scientist in the study of linguistics and human evolution. In addition to conducting experiments on human subjects, Rose also publishes peer-reviewed essays and distributes self-published analyses on animal behavior. Her most recent studies examine the concept of '*umwelt*', first developed by theorist Jakob von Uexküll. Rose's highly anticipated essay on the topic will be released in May of 2013, and is entitled: "The Cognitive Complications of the Speciest."

OTHER PUBLICATIONS

AB, 2010

PROXEMICS, 2010

ON OBJECTIVITY, 2010

ANTHRO, 2011

ISS EXPERIMENTAL ARCHIVE, 2011

**RESCUE
+PRESS**